11 Ways to JumpStart Your Thinking

Change Your Mindset to Achieve the Success You Deserve

JaQuette M. S. Gilbert

Copyright © 2015 JaQuette Gilbert

All rights reserved.

This book may not be reproduced in whole or in part, in any form or by any means, electronic or mechanical, including photocopying, recording, or by any information storage and retrieval system now known or hereafter invented without written permission from the publisher.

ISBN-13: **978-0692575703**

ISBN-10: **0692575707**

DEDICATION

This book is dedicated to every ambitious go-getter. You may sometimes doubt that your dreams will ever become a reality, but I wrote this book to give you hope. You can do anything you want to do. I believe in you! ☺

CONTENTS

	Acknowledgments	I
	Introduction	3
Chapter 1	Who Do You Think You Are?	6
Chapter 2	Free Your Mind	14
Chapter 3	What's Really Blocking You?	20
Chapter 4	I'm All Ears	25
Chapter 5	You Are What You Speak	32
Chapter 6	Reading Is Fundamental	38
Chapter 7	It's Not That Serious—or Is It?	46
Chapter 8	Think and Act on Purpose	52
Chapter 9	Did I Do That?	62
Chapter 10	Hi. I'm a Recovering Perfectionist.	70
Chapter 11	Can't Stop, Won't Stop	75
	Conclusion	81

ACKNOWLEDGMENTS

I would like to thank God for giving me the inspiration to write this book. I am not perfect, but I am thankful for my journey, and I am thankful for the opportunity to help others attain success.

I would also like to thank my wonderful husband, Gregory Gilbert, for pushing me to finish this book. I appreciate the encouragement and support you gave me. I couldn't have done this without you. I love you!

There are so many others who played a role in my journey to publishing my first book. Kevin Brown, thank you for showing me that I was in fact that servant who was cowardly hiding her talent the Master had entrusted to her.

Thank you Loren Chestnut for researching, making contacts for me, and being an awesome sounding board.

Thank you to my editor, Ken, book cover designer, Vikiana, and everyone else who gave me tips and encouragement along the way—you know who you are! ☺

INTRODUCTION

What comes to mind when you hear the word "jumpstart"? For me, I think of a car battery that has temporarily lost its ability to function properly. Well, your mind is similar to a car battery. Sometimes, after going so many miles in life, you lose the energy or momentum needed to reach your goal. You had so many hopes and dreams, only to find your life is not even close to where you had imagined you would be. What happened? Why haven't you reached the level of success you wanted? Why haven't you reached your goals?

Does any of this sound familiar? It does to me. Despite having a "good job" and a loving family, I felt like I was running out of steam. I wasn't truly happy with my life, and didn't feel very successful. Little did I know that I was actually the one responsible for the lack of fulfillment in my life.

I later discovered that there were things in my environment that I allowed to negatively shape my thought process. I allowed myself to be fed by what others said, what I read, what I watched on television, and even by my own negative words. Have you ever heard the saying, "You are what you eat"? Well, when you surround yourself with negativity, it makes it more difficult to achieve success. However, when you surround yourself with positive people and things, you have no choice but to walk in your greatness. It is amazing how much your mindset can shift when you change your surroundings.

You may want to achieve more but not know how. Maybe you don't know your purpose or your passion. It is my hope that, after reading this book, you will be one step closer to understanding how your surroundings shape your thought process. I want you to know why you are here, and how you can use your gift to make your dream a reality. I want you to know that your definition of success may differ from others, and that is completely fine. You cannot make everyone happy, and you shouldn't try to do so.

This book is not intended to make you get rich quick or even to make you an overnight success. This book is intended, however, to show you that life is a puzzle. It is your job to gain clarity about how each puzzle piece works to make you better. It is also your job to strategize the best way to put each piece together so you can achieve the success you deserve. Know that the lessons you learn along the way will help mold you into the person you were designed to be. Enjoy the process. Enjoy the journey.

In this book, we will explore eleven ways to jumpstart your thinking. At the end of each chapter is a self-check guide, as well as a call to action. To maximize the gains from each of these sections, I urge you to reflect and respond to each question, and to complete each call to action activity as honestly as you can. Write down your responses so you can reflect on your growth at a later time. I have included an overview of each of the eleven ways to jumpstart your thinking below.

✓ Know who you are, and know your worth.

- ✓ Free your mind by engaging in prayer and meditation.

- ✓ Identify your success blockers and ways to combat them.

- ✓ Be aware of who and what you listen to.

- ✓ Engage in positive conversation and avoid speaking negatively about your past, present and future circumstances.

- ✓ Read books and articles that will add value to your life.

- ✓ Be aware of how television and movies shape your thinking.

- ✓ Think and act on purpose.

- ✓ Be accountable.

- ✓ Let go of perfectionism.

- ✓ Don't give up.

Now that you know what's in store, buckle up, and brace yourself for the journey ahead! Here's to believing in you!

1 WHO DO YOU THINK YOU ARE?

Unless you know who you are, you will always be vulnerable to what people say.
-Dr. Phil McGraw

Do you know who you are? Or is your perception of yourself based on what others have said about you? It's a scary thing not to know who you are. If you want to be successful and develop a positive mindset, you have to be sure of who you are and who you are not. Otherwise, other people can easily mold you into who they want you to be.

Supermodel Tyra Banks is a great example of someone who did not allow anyone else to define who she should be. Tyra struggled initially to get into the modeling world. She was met with comments such as, "We already have a black model," and, "You're too ethnic." When Tyra finally landed a contract with Elite Model Management, she booked more runway show contracts in a week than your typical newbie. Yet, when Tyra gained weight, she chose to return to modeling in the States. Some modeling professionals in Europe apparently did not feel her new shape was flattering or appealing. But you know what? Tyra was determined to feel comfortable in her skin. She refused to starve herself to fit the definition of beauty that others had concocted. Tyra didn't need anyone to tell her who she was—she already knew.

What about you? Do you feel like you can be yourself? I know you have dreams and goals, but before you set out to conquer the world, I want you to make sure you are absolutely sure of who you are. Why? It's because the journey you are about to begin will be rough at times. In these moments, some may question you. They may try to make you believe you are not "the school type" or that you are not "the business type". If you are not sure of your identity, you may give up on your destiny simply because of what naysayers say to you.

You Were Meant to Be Here

Have you ever really taken the time to sit back and think about how you came into existence? My husband and I were talking about this, and he opened up my eyes to some truths I had not considered. I never really thought about it in the way my husband explained it, but it makes so much sense. It truly is an awesome thing to be alive, when you consider the battle each of us endured to get here.

One of the first things you need to do to achieve success and jumpstart your thinking is to know you were meant to be here. You have to believe you were sent to be here at this particular time, in this present moment. You've heard about miracle babies, right? Well, you were a miracle baby. You were destined to be here. How is this possible? According to my husband, you have to think about it in terms of the "conception process". Now, I will try to keep this as PG as possible.

During the process that leads up to conception, there are millions of tiny, little "soldiers" that march around the field. They all have a goal in mind, which is to reach a prize at the end—the "golden egg" if you will. So many "soldiers" try with all their might to reach that prize, but there can only be one that is successful (generally speaking anyway). It's a tough journey, but there's one soldier that presses on and says, "I'm going to win. I'm going to get the golden egg." That, my friend, is the solider that wins the race. That solider is you.

You see, you were a fighter before you even got here. I know you may be struggling with finding "more" out of life. It's only fair that you give life a chance. It's only fair that you continue to fight and find out what your purpose is, and why you are here. Trust me, you really were destined to be here.

I know there are a lot of clichés out there. Some say, "There's only one you," or, "No one else can be you." Sometimes we hear those clichés so many times that we tend to overlook the truth behind them. The truth is that there really is only one you. Only one person can do your job, and that is *you*.

There are people assigned to each and every one of us. We are responsible for helping these individuals get to their next level in life. Your life, the words you say, and the things you do, all of these things are not just to make you happy. There is a bigger purpose. Your purpose goes far beyond what you could ever imagine. Your purpose goes beyond you. You were meant to touch the lives of others.

Stop Seeking Approval!

An amazing thing happens when you stop seeking

approval and validation: You find it. People are naturally drawn like magnets to those who know who they are and cannot be shaken!

-Mandy Hall, *The Single Woman: Life, Love, and a Dash of Sass*

In order to jumpstart your thinking, you have to remember how valuable you are—not just to yourself, but to the world. You are extremely valuable. You are unique. You are exquisite. I urge you to take the time you need to understand your worth.

When you know who you are, you don't need to wait on someone else to give you permission to follow your dreams. You have the authority to devise a strategy to achieve your goals. Why? It's your life. You must live your life for you. You may want to seek counseling occasionally for certain things in life, and that is okay. Everyone needs reassurance at times. However, you should not be afraid to make a move without someone else's approval.

Did you know that your demeanor teaches others how to perceive you? If you are unsure of yourself, how can others take you seriously? If you do not believe in yourself or value yourself, why should anyone else? Your confidence in your identity commands the same confidence from others. Make sure you are modeling the right expectations.

The Comparing Game

When we watch television or look inside magazines, we see a lot of people who seem to have "arrived". For instance, there are many celebrities who make life seem so glitzy and glamorous. If you're not careful, you can find yourself saying, "Gosh, I wish my life was as awesome as theirs," or "Why can't I have the life that they have? Don't I deserve to have the best that life offers?" The answer to your question is, "Yes." Yes, you do deserve to have the best that life offers. However, what is it that makes you feel you must compare your life to that of others? What makes others seem more valuable?

When you compare yourself to someone else, you don't realize that you are actually declaring there is something wrong with you. You are declaring you have a deficiency that makes you less valuable. You are saying you must live in the shadows of someone else in order to increase your worth. There is such a danger in comparing yourself to others. You can lose yourself completely and find yourself doing things you never would have imagined.

You do not know what it took someone to get to their current place in life, so it really isn't fair to compare your life to someone else's. The funny thing is as you are comparing yourself to others, someone is comparing their life to yours. There is someone out there right now who sees so much potential and so much value in you that they want to emulate you. Funny how that works, huh?

Oftentimes, we disregard and play down our strengths, our good qualities and our talents because, in our eyes, it's not good enough, it's not as good as someone else. We may be averaging fifteen points per basketball game, but it's not as good as MJ or Kobe Bryant. So we end up feeling inadequate and less valuable than others. I urge you to stop comparing yourself to others. Instead, look within yourself and accept yourself for who you are. Your strengths and limitations set you apart from others.

I can remember looking at one of my friends and admiring her talent and creativity. I have no idea how she comes up with so many great ideas. I even thought about how much more valuable my life would be if I had creative juices like hers. The funny thing is that, one day, she told me that, although she had so much creativity bottled up inside of her, she wished she had my drive. How crazy is that? I would have never guessed it because she certainly had the total package in my opinion. I was stunned that I could have something that someone else wanted. In that moment, I realized that measuring our worth and success against that of others is a disservice to us. By engaging in the "comparing game" we overshadow our worth.

You Have What It Takes

The person you most admire has their own share of testimonies. Sometimes, they wanted to give up, too. You see, oftentimes when we compare ourselves to others, we don't consider the journey it took those individuals to reach their current place in life. We cannot look at where someone else currently is in life and compare it to where we are today. That line of thinking is unfair to both parties. You did not both take the same path in life. We all have our own journey, our own trials, and our own temptations. We stumble, and we fall. This does not take away from our value. Instead, it reminds us that we are human.

You have everything you need inside of you to successfully develop a positive mindset and lifestyle. You may have trouble remembering this some days (I'm guilty of forgetting this some days, too). It's hard to do this sometimes when you focus only on what's right in front of you. For example, you could be working a mediocre, low-paying job today. Yet, within the next two years, you could very well become the

CEO of your own company. It may seem unreachable initially, but with the right planning, determination, and mindset, you can definitely achieve anything you set your mind to. You must see beyond your current circumstances.

It's easy to look at the success of someone else, and to think that their lifestyle comes without a price. Success is not instant. This may be a hard concept to fully grasp because we live in a society where instant gratification seems like a necessity. We want instant food, instant cash, and instant status. We often fail to consider the cost of instant gratification. Sometimes, you actually end up missing out on some very valuable lessons that you would have learned had you not taken the fast track on your journey. In addition to being goal-oriented, you should embrace the journey and the mistakes that come along with it. This is what makes you unique. This is what shapes your character and builds you up.

Self-Check Guide

Finding out who you are is an important step to improving your mindset.

1. List three to five words to describe yourself.

2. On a scale of 1 to 10, how valuable do you think you are (with 10 being the highest)?

3. Who do you compare yourself to?

4. What qualities make this person/these people seem more valuable than you?

5. What value do you see in yourself?

6. When do you feel inadequate? In what areas?

7. What can you do to improve your perception of yourself?

Call to Action

Make a list of your skills and talents. Dig deep and be honest with yourself as you complete this activity. Do not water down or downplay your gifts. List all of your skills or talents on a sheet of paper. Was your list surprising? Now brainstorm ways your skills add value to the lives of others.

2 FREE YOUR MIND

Meditation is not a way of making your mind quiet. It's a way of entering into the quiet that's already there – buried under the 50,000 thoughts the average person thinks every day.
-Deepak Chopra

It can be difficult to achieve success and to jump-start your thinking when you have so many thoughts running through your mind—trust me, I can relate! Before moving on in your journey, you need to clear your mind of all negative thoughts. How can you do this? Through prayer and meditation. You cannot expect to overcome a negative mindset until you free your mind. You may not consider yourself an inherently negative person, but everyone suffers from negative thoughts at some time or another. You must work daily to free yourself of poisonous, dead weights and thoughts. How can you do this? You can do so by beginning and ending each day with prayer and meditation.

Although I encourage you to pray and meditate on good, positive thoughts continuously throughout your day, it is undeniable that beginning and ending your day with an intentional positive mindset makes a huge difference. You should choose a quiet setting in the morning and at night in order to decrease your chances of being disturbed. If you have a family or small children, you may want to wake up a little earlier than normal to ensure you have sufficient time for prayer and meditation. This may be a difficult feat for some; however, it is all about priorities and doing what works best for you. Don't fret if you cannot do mornings consistently. I am a mom of three, and I know how rough some mornings can be. Yet, if I cannot get my prayer time in (or as much as I'd like) before everyone wakes up, I still manage to find a few minutes later in my morning. I have learned over time that rearranging in lieu of complaining works better. However, I didn't always have this mind frame.

After the birth of each of my three daughters, I was very overwhelmed, needless to say. Both my mother and mother-in-law came to help take care of my first daughter. Each of these incredible women stayed with my husband and me for one week. This was a huge help to us! It gave us time to breathe a little bit. After my second daughter was born, my mother and grandmother came to visit us at the hospital. Yet after the birth of my youngest daughter, we did not have any family members to help. The logic, I guess, was that if I survived motherhood that far, clearly I did not need any help. This was far from the truth!

What I learned from this experience is that sometimes we may need to ask, beg, or plead for help from our family and loved ones. It is our job to communicate our needs with others. It could be that your inner circle is unaware of your struggles, and would gladly provide assistance if they knew you needed it.

As I mentioned before, if your obligations restrict your time for prayer and meditation then you can seek alternative times that work. The morning or night may not work for you, but you should still seek to find the best time that does. If you have a significant other, s/he may be able to alleviate you briefly to accommodate your quiet time.

You may be wondering how long you should pray or meditate. Initially, you may only be able to dedicate five minutes towards prayer and meditation, and that is fine. You may be able to dedicate more time as your schedule allows in the future. The point is you must value yourself enough to even do it. My motto is: quality versus quantity!

To be quite honest, there are some days when I oversleep or "life happens", and I must quickly get my children and myself ready for our day. When this happens, I may or may not have time to follow my normal prayer and meditation routine. Therefore, I say a brief prayer, and get my children to school. Once that is done, I have more time to settle down and read, pray, and meditate. Even if I am unable to follow my normal routine, I make sure to set aside time in my day to get centered. You are worth setting aside time for, too. This helps to maximize your potential.

Again, don't fret if your morning (or night) doesn't go as planned. Just be sure to find a few minutes to yourself at some point throughout your day. Like I mentioned before, I'm not always able to have as much time as I'd like some days, but I still make up for it at a time that's better.

Ultimately, it is your choice to implement this strategy as a part of your daily life. Each choice you make affects your future.

Benefits of Prayer and Meditation

Meditation is listening to the Divine within.
-Edgar Cayce

There are many benefits of prayer and meditation. One of the benefits is that they can reduce stress. When you learn to free your mind, your body will release the toxic, negative energy that likes to keep you from progressing and achieving success. Another benefit is that prayer and meditation can reveal clarity in various circumstances that occur in your life.

Prayer and meditation are about seeking wholeness and a connection to a power that is greater than you. For me, prayer and meditation are necessary because I realize that I cannot do life alone. I must seek solace, comfort and guidance from God. Only He can direct my path. I do understand that not everyone may share in my religious beliefs, and that is quite okay. I would never try to force my beliefs on anyone. I am simply saying that prayer and meditation are especially necessary on my journey to success. You may find the same is true for you, too. Prayer and meditation are also quite helpful when you decide to embrace a positive lifestyle.

There are different methods of meditation that work well for some, but not for others. For example, some people choose to read scriptures from biblical or religious texts while others choose to engage in Yoga, walking, running, or some other form of exercise. Your method of meditation may differ from that of someone else. Sometimes when I meditate I like to intentionally think about positive, encouraging thoughts. At other times I prefer to sit in silence, and listen for guidance. Soft music often helps me during this time.

Meditation is simply amazing because it allows you to think more clearly. Meditation helps you free yourself from negative forces that attack your mind. It also helps you to accept the positive energy surrounding you. If you are serious about wanting to jumpstart your thinking, I urge you to develop and maintain a life filled with consistent prayer and meditation.

Self-Check Guide

Think about your prayer/meditation life and answer the following questions:

1) How often do you pray and/or meditate?

2) How does prayer/meditation affect your life currently?

3) How do you plan to incorporate prayer or meditation into your daily life if you're not currently doing so?

Call to Action

Begin and end your day with prayer/meditation for the next five days. If you are unable to spend fifteen or twenty minutes then dedicate five or ten minutes to prayer and/or meditation each day. Remember, quality is more important than quantity. You may choose to focus on a specific area in your life to pray or meditate about. During this special time, expect good changes to come about as a result of your dedication. Record your reflections about this experience daily. Describe how this experience makes you feel, as well as the gains of being consistent and dedicated.

3 WHAT'S REALLY BLOCKING YOU?

You will find what you're looking for.
-Craig Groeschel

I was listening to a sermon on YouTube one day. The pastor speaking was Craig Groeschel, and he was talking about reasons to be optimistic. Although he was speaking from more of a spiritual standpoint, he said something that I think everyone could agree upon. He described the difference between a vulture (or buzzard) and a hummingbird. Vultures search primarily for dead animals to devour while hummingbirds look for something sweet. The result is the same for both birds; they both find what they are looking for.

You can apply this same logic to your life. Maybe you have a dream of becoming a doctor or opening your own law firm. You can choose to think of your dream in one of two ways. Like the vulture, you can search for all of the reasons why you don't think you will ever achieve your dream. These are usually easier to come up with. You may think you're too old, not smart enough or that it will take too much of a risk to go for your dream. Alternatively, you could choose to be like the hummingbird. Although you acknowledge difficulties around you, you choose to search for the reasons why you will make your dream a reality anyway.

It's like the old "is the glass half empty or half full" question. Choosing to see your life as "lacking" or "deficient" may make you anxious about your ability to reach your goal. However, when you choose to adopt the "half full" mentality, you can have fewer apprehensions about your success. Although you may not have all of the right tools right now (i.e. finances, network), this "half full" perspective can give you enough encouragement to successfully finish the race. You have the choice to embrace or dismiss negative thoughts. If you choose to embrace them, you are guaranteeing that your future will be as dead as the carrion enjoyed by vultures. Yet, if you choose to focus on the positive, you will be on your way to developing a sweet and satisfying future.

Success Blockers

Create the highest, grandest vision possible for your life because you become what you believe.
-Oprah Winfrey

As you embark on your journey to reach your goal, you may encounter things that try to stop you from gaining success. One of these success blockers might be your mindset. Let's face it. Even the toughest person has moments of doubt—even if it only lasts briefly. In order to reach your goal, you must continuously work on developing a positive mindset. Without a positive mindset, you will live your life like the vulture we talked about earlier.

Sometimes you may be tempted to entertain irrational fears, negative thoughts, doubts, and even give in to procrastination. These are all success blockers. They can affect your self-esteem, and make it difficult to achieve your goal. If you aren't careful, you may feel you don't have what it takes or that you are not worthy of your intended success. Don't give in to these success blockers!

You may be wondering how you can overcome these success blockers. First, you must dismiss them. Do not accept them as truth or as indicators of inevitable failure. Then you must intentionally replace these poisonous thoughts with uplifting ones. Do not be discouraged if you struggle to embrace the positive at first. In many cases, it took years to develop negative thought patterns, so it is no wonder that the road to developing a positive mindset requires persistence. Hang in there! I believe you can achieve victory in every area of your life, simply by conquering every success blocker head on.

Who are you living for?

Stop doing what's acceptable. Start doing what's your purpose.
-Maya Elious

You may have placed a dream on the back burner because of what others think you should be doing. You probably told them what you want to do, but they politely suggested you should go another route. Although most people mean well, they don't always realize that they could be pushing their negative thoughts on to you. If you're not careful, you may begin to embrace their unbelief. You start thinking you should just do what everyone around you thinks is right for you. You may already know that their advice doesn't align with your purpose, but you give in because you don't want to rock the boat. This is another success blocker—being a people pleaser.

As difficult as it may be, you cannot allow the fear of disappointing others to stop you from achieving your success. If you want to be successful, you have to move beyond doing what's acceptable all the time. Move towards doing what makes you happy. Take Bill Gates, for example. Bill Gates went to Harvard with the intention of being a lawyer like his dad. However, he could not escape his passion: technology. To his parents' dismay, he dropped out of school to pursue his passion. Now, his parents may not have understood why he would "throw away" such a perfect opportunity to get the best education. Think about it. Computers were not the big thing yet, so you can understand why his parents may have had their doubts. Yet, like Bill Gates, you must decide who you're living for. Will you embrace the doubts and fears of others or will you work to defy the odds, and make your dream a reality?

Self-Check Guide

You may be struggling right now with a huge decision. Should you go for your dream or should you play it safe? Reflect on what you learned in this chapter as you answer each question.

1) Who are you living for?

2) Are you happy with how things are going in your life?

3) What's blocking you from achieving the success you want?

4) What steps can you take to overcome the "success blockers" in your life?

Call to Action

People love giving advice—even when they don't have all the facts! Maybe you have expressed your dreams to a friend or loved one, and they don't agree. That's okay. Sometimes we do need a reality check, at other times we need to stick to our guns. It's your job to figure out when you need to accept or reject advice from others.

Right now, I want you to make a list of the things everyone else has told you that you should consider doing. What are the benefits of doing each of those things? Will you have financial freedom? Security? 401K? Now, make a list of your dreams. What is the benefit in following your heart? Success is measured by what we think. Both lists are examples of successful lifestyles. Which one are you going to choose?

4 I'M ALL EARS

I like to listen. I have learned a great deal from listening carefully. Most people never listen.
   -Ernest Hemingway

On your road to success, you must be careful about the things you listen to. Why? Because your thoughts and beliefs are shaped by what you listen to. If you listen to negative garbage, it will be very difficult to walk into your greatness. You cannot have a positive mindset if you are constantly filling your ears with negativity, lies, doubts, and fears.

I can remember being a young child and wondering why it seemed like my parents were so mean and too different some days. In my mind, they were the only ones who would not allow their children to listen to any music except gospel. Now don't get me wrong; I absolutely love gospel music. There is simply nothing quite like it. I love the message that I hear in many gospel songs, and I love the sounds; however, this did not stop me from believing my parents were robbing me of a normal, typical childhood. I felt like an outsider when my friends knew the latest songs on the radio and the latest dances. Heck, I didn't even know any of the oldies! To my peers, I was just "the church girl". I now know there are far worse things to be called!

I can appreciate what my parents were trying to do for me now that I'm older. They were simply teaching me the importance of being cautious in what I listened to. I couldn't understand this vital lesson as a child, but I am so grateful for this teaching at this point in my life. Let's take songs, for example. You see, when you listen to songs, it is almost as if you are automatically entranced by the music. We generally do not listen for the lyrics of any song initially. Instead, we listen to the beat and to the arrangement of the sounds. This is not necessarily a bad thing because instruments are wonderful. Music is amazing, and it can completely take you out of this world. Yet, sometimes, when we focus on the sounds that are produced, it can be difficult to focus on the lyrics or the message the song carries.

It's kind of funny that I turned out like my parents after all—focusing on the lyrics of songs that is. I have found in my experience that the lyrics of songs can change my mood, thoughts, and behaviors. My husband and I were discussing this topic one day, and I realized he felt the same way. He told me he used to absolutely love listening to a certain rapper when he was younger. Yet he noticed his mood would change, and he would become angry after listening to some of this particular artist's songs. He later realized the lyrics of the songs promoted anger and violence. It's crazy how much of an effect songs can have on us.

I have always loved music. In fact, I come from a musical family. Although my family only allowed me to listen to gospel music, I admit I fell in love with pop after I started attending boarding school. I did notice a change in myself at times though. After listening to certain songs several times, it became easier to tolerate and justify beliefs that were contrary to my moral compass. For example, I remember when the song "Follow Me" by Uncle Kracker was new. The music is oh, so catchy, and the harmony is great. Yet I listened to a speaker at chapel one day who pointed out that the song actually went against the teachings of the Bible. The song talks about how we should be okay with cheating on our spouse because of the connection we may have with someone else—this is clearly not an appropriate thing to do!

Now, you may be thinking I have gone off the deep end, and you may be saying I can't blame the cheating scandals of today on songs. Trust me. I am not saying music is the sole source of influence on our actions, but I am saying it would be unwise to pour inappropriate thoughts into our mind. These thoughts do not need room to grow into something that could hurt us or others around us! If you want to be successful and to develop more of a positive mindset then you must consider what you are listening to. If what you are listening to does not add value to your life or goes against your moral judgment, you may need to reconsider listening to it. Thoughts produce beliefs, and beliefs produce actions.

Everyone Will Not Support You

If you want to be successful, prepare to be doubted and tested. -Unknown

Words are so powerful. They are something that you cannot take back—ever! As I alluded to earlier in this book, you must also be careful about *who* you are listening to if you ever want to be successful or jump-start your thinking. Not everyone has your best interest at heart. If you have a dream inside of you not everyone wants to hear about it. That may sound harsh, but it is the cold, hard truth.

You may very well want to share your excitement about your plans with everyone you meet; however, there will be many who will strive to crush your spirit. Some will do this unintentionally, while others will do it deliberately. Think about it. Let's say you just bought a new car. Instead of being happy for you, your co-worker decides to buy a vehicle that is more expensive. Or maybe your family questions why you didn't choose to purchase a car in a different price range. Everyone has their own opinions and perspectives. You cannot allow the beliefs of others to cause you to abandon your mission or to feel badly about achieving or progressing towards your goals.

The truth is some individuals do not want you to prosper simply because they have not reached their goals. This line of thinking assumes that if they are not happy then you shouldn't be happy either. Crazy, right? As crazy as this sounds, there are so many who begin to doubt the necessity of their dream simply because of something someone said to them. These individuals may have a burning desire to open a business, change careers, or whatever their heart desires, yet because "Uncle Jim" or "Cousin Sally" couldn't keep their businesses afloat, they don't think it is even worth it for you to try your hand at entrepreneurship.

Oftentimes, we speak about our goals with those who do not have the knowledge base to assist us. As helpful and as loving as these individuals may be, they can sometimes deter us from our mission by their lack of understanding and encouragement. If you are going to successfully jumpstart your thinking, you must listen to the wisdom of those with expertise in your area of interest.

Following the advice of someone without expertise in your area of interest is not what's best for you. Yet, some *choose* to listen to the words of individuals who are not even qualified to coach or give assistance to someone with their particular interests. Notice the word "choose". We all have choices. As wrong as someone may be for pouring out negative vibes, it is equally wrong for you to *accept* the negativity as truth. You have a gift to share with your community, your state, your country, and even the world. Yet, if you choose to embrace negative words from others, you will never be able to jumpstart your thinking, and you will never know the potential your vision could have on the lives of others.

I have always enjoyed writing. When I was a little girl, I wanted to become a writer. However, I was told that wasn't necessarily the best path for me because I wouldn't make a lot of money. Although I can see (and appreciate) the intent behind this statement, I wish it was packaged differently, you know? Instead of encouraging me to write *in addition* to doing something else, I felt the need to completely abandon my love of writing. Why? Well, everyone else thought it would keep me from getting to where I needed to be in life—financially speaking.

This thought process happens to a lot of us. We abandon our goals because we listened to what someone said about our plans. Fortunately, I have learned how to incorporate writing into my day. I enjoy writing down inspirational quotes and personal reflections, and I have even turned my hand to blogging. I know you can find ways to incorporate your passions into your schedule, too. If you are going to achieve success and jumpstart your thinking, you must guard your mind against negative talk from others—well intentioned or not.

Self-Check Guide

This activity should help you take inventory of who and what you listen to, as well as how these individuals and things affect your mindset. The more honest you are with yourself the more you will benefit from doing this activity.

Before beginning, it is important that you note the difference between a dream and a goal. Earlier in this book, you compared your dreams to what others believe you should do with your life. A dream is simply a wish or a thought. You don't necessarily have to take action. Dreams only require you to have an imagination about what life *could* look like.

Goals are different from dreams because they are time-sensitive and require action on your part. Goals force you to plan and are measurable. You can analyze the results of your actions and use that data to make even better strategies to achieve your goal. Now that you understand the difference between a dream and a goal, please read and complete the questions below.

1. List your goals. You may list personal development and/or business goals. Be specific. Example: I want to be debt-free by June 30, 2018.

2. Have you ever shared these goals with anyone? If not, why haven't you shared your ambitions?

3. If you have told others about your dream, what were the responses from each person you told? How did their responses change your opinion of your goals?

4. Think about the types of songs, podcasts, Periscope streams, television shows, and movies you listen to or watch. Do these things add value to your life? Are they eliciting positive messages to

uplift you?

Call to Action

Look at your current movie and song collections. If you do not own physical DVDs or CDs (gasp!), simply think of the kinds of movies and songs you entertain on Hulu, Netflix, Pandora, or whatever medium you use. Do these movies and songs encourage the new, optimistic perspective you want to develop? If not, decide what steps you want to take so you can begin to eliminate these negative items from your life.

Now, I want you think of a motivational or inspirational person. Some of my favorites are Oprah and John Maxwell. Feel free to choose whoever you like. If you need to do research, that is fine. Remember, Google and YouTube are your friends! Your task is to find podcasts, interviews, or audio books from this person. For the next week, listen to your audio selection(s). In your journal or notebook, write down statements that resonate with you. Reflect on your notes throughout the week. The purpose of these activities is:

1) To teach you to pay attention to what you entertain.

2) To show how listening to motivational or inspiring words (repeatedly) can change your mood, thought patterns, actions, and life.

In order to jumpstart your thinking, you must *intentionally* listen to optimistic individuals. You must feed your mind words that will build you up where you are weak, not those which continue to tear you down. You must commit to protecting your mind from accepting negative talk—from yourself and from others. These activities will show you how possible it is for you to jump-start your thinking.

5 YOU ARE WHAT YOU SPEAK

Whether you think you can or you think you can't, you're right.
-Henry Ford

As I mentioned before, words are extremely powerful. If you want to be successful and jumpstart your thinking, you must be very careful about the words that proceed from your mouth. The Bible tells us that there is life and death in the tongue. To me, this means that I have the power to change my destiny based on the words that I speak over my life. Can you imagine the kind of life you could have if you only spoke it into existence? Of course, in addition to speaking positively, you need to engage in appropriate, intentional actions that will allow you to achieve your goals.

It is so essential to remember that your thoughts affect your beliefs, and your beliefs affect your actions. For example, you may be trying to lose weight. If you tell yourself you will never be able to lose 50 pounds then guess what will happen. You will not be able to lose the weight! It is amazing how our mind operates. Speaking positively is sort of like our secret weapon. It can give us the energy we need to make our goals and dreams a reality.

It doesn't matter how bleak the situation may appear, if you continue to speak positively, you are bound to achieve your goals. I can remember looking at the course assignments for one of my play therapy courses, and wondering how in the world I would be able to write a 50 page manual in addition to the regular assignments each week. Did I mention my husband's job had relocated him to another site out of state during this time? So, in addition to being a full-time student and teacher, I was also responsible for caring for my three daughters. Had I chosen to tell myself that it was simply impossible for me to take on this workload, I would have never known the inner strength I possessed. I was able to successfully complete all of my required readings and assignments in addition to the 50 page manual.

You see, success does not come from simply speaking a goal *one time*. You have to continuously speak positive things in your life in order to see the necessary changes come to pass. This is how you are able to be successful and to jumpstart your thinking. Trials will come, but you must persevere by continuing to speak positively—regardless of your current circumstances. I strongly suggest you consider writing and speaking affirmations for your life.

An affirmation is simply a positive or encouraging statement in which you are affirming something specific about your life. Notice, I said "specific". If you want to jumpstart your thinking, you must learn to speak specifically and intentionally into your life. You cannot believe vague statements will get you to where you want to go. For example, instead of saying, "I will write a book one day," you should say, "I will complete my book by August 3, 2016." Do you see the difference between both statements? The first statement did not give a clear indication of when you wanted to have your book completed. When you speak specifically and intentionally, you have a clearer vision of exactly what you desire to come to pass. This makes it easier to hold yourself accountable for your success or lack thereof.

Verbalizing Affirmations

Verbalizing positive statements is an essential component to jumpstarting your thinking. Earlier, I mentioned how it is necessary to write a list of affirmations. Reading these statements every day will help shift your mindset into the right direction. Yet you would be amazed at how affirming it is to say each statement aloud. Although you may not initially believe what you are saying, prolonged exposure to your affirmations will cause you to eventually change your negative mindset. If you have extreme difficulty believing in your affirmations, you may need to question whether you are being honest with what you truly want. This may not be the case for everyone, but it can be quite difficult to achieve success if you do not believe in yourself or your ability to make your dream a reality. You need to work to the point where you can actually envision yourself living out every word from your list of affirmations. If you wrote that you attract money everywhere you go then you need to actually see your bank account balance increasing as you speak.

Verbalizing my affirmations has been such a blessing to my life. For example, at the beginning of every quarter in graduate school, I would pray for clarity and the ability to maintain a great GPA. I can recall saying aloud, "I will make an A in this course." No matter how difficult and challenging my life was, I always believed I would earn an A in whatever course I pursued. And guess what? God honored my prayers! To me, when I say my affirmations aloud, it is almost as if I am sealing the deal on my fate. It gives me the extra confidence I need to get the ball rolling or to complete a specific task.

You may be wondering how often to verbalize your affirmations. Ideally, it is best to recite them at least twice each day—once in the morning, and once at night.

Why? It's a great way to begin and end your day. It's perfectly okay if you find you need to say your affirmations multiple times throughout the day. You are training yourself to focus on positive images regardless of your current circumstances. If you are having an exceptionally difficult time during the day, you may recite them during these moments so you can regain your focus.

When We Fall Down

It can be quite difficult to speak positively all the time. We are human, and we all have our moments—good and bad. Yet this does not in any way excuse our behavior, nor does it give us a license to intentionally speak negatively. There is a simple exercise that I apply to my life and have encouraged my daughters to try as well. If you say something negative, you must then counter your negative statement with two positive ones. Your positive statements can be about any topic of your choice. For example, "I am thankful to be alive today," or "I am grateful to have a jacket to keep me warm in this weather."

Your statements are a reminder to be content with where you are in the present moment, and they also serve as a way to regain control of your focus. Why should you say two positive statements instead of one? By saying only one positive statement you are simply canceling the one negative statement. However, our goal is to overcome negative thinking. Multiple positive statements help achieve this. The more positive you are, the more likely it is that you will achieve your goals.

Self-Check Guide

Reflect on what you learned in this chapter, and be honest as you answer the questions below.

1. Do you struggle with speaking negatively?

2. Have you ever written affirmations? If so, do you read them aloud? Have they been beneficial to you?

3. Think about your goals. What positive statements can you begin saying about them?

4. Do you find yourself intentionally making positive statements? If not, give it a try, and see how this new perspective changes your mood!

Call to Action

For the next week, I want you to reflect on the conversations you have with others. Use a notepad to identify positive statements that you say as well as those others say to you. Then identify negative statements that you and others make during your conversations. How did you feel after hearing the positive statements? What about the negative ones? The purpose of this activity is two-fold:

1) To teach you how necessary it is to intentionally speak in a positive manner.

2) To help you identify the kinds of individuals with whom you associate.

In order to be successful and to jumpstart your thinking, you must *intentionally* speak life into your circumstances, and those around you must do the same.

You must also work diligently to protect your goals. This activity will help you decrease your chances of self-sabotage, as well as minimize the chances of you allowing others to negatively influence your line of thinking.

6 READING IS FUNDAMENTAL

*The more that you read, the more things you will know.
The more you learn, the more places you'll go!*
   -Dr. Seuss

We've established that, if you're ever going to reach your goal, you need to jumpstart your thinking. We've also gone over several tips you can use to replace your negative mindset. By now, you're probably thinking there couldn't be anything else to do, right? Wrong! Another thing you need to do is begin or increase your reading habits.

I know what you're thinking. You don't have enough time, your reading days ended with your last English course, you don't really enjoy reading, and reading can't really help you. I used to think some of these things, too. Boy, was I wrong. What I found out is that there are interests I developed as a result of reading, and I gained a wealth of knowledge I never knew existed. It's funny how you don't know what you don't know until you begin reading!

As a child, I got into trouble often because, instead of sleeping, I would use the hallway light to read. To this day, my mother believes I have poor vision because of my nightly reading. Unfortunately, I lost some enthusiasm for reading during my college years. I just couldn't get into many of the assigned readings. In graduate school, I had similar experiences until I found out about play therapy. I became hooked. I started reading as many articles as I could find on the subject, and even ended up taking a certificate program in play therapy. Just think. I never would have known about play therapy if I had never read about it's amazing benefits.

Do I really have to read?

Do you have to include reading in your schedule? No, but if you want to develop a positive mindset and reach your goals, you must purposefully do things that will benefit you—especially when you don't want to. Changing your habits to include reading can be difficult, but it's certainly not impossible. With the right planning and an awesome support system in place, you will be one step closer to successfully jumpstarting your thinking and achieving your goals.

You may be wondering how you can add one more thing to your to-do list. Like you, I have a full schedule. Yet I have been able to jumpstart my thinking by intentionally planning time to read. Simply put, I make it a priority in my life. When I pick up my older daughters from school, I usually arrive early enough to sneak in about twenty minutes or so of reading. Why? I have less distractions since my youngest usually naps during this time.

You may have more or less time to dedicate to reading. The key is to start. Look at your schedule. When can you feasibly add a little (more) reading time? While you're waiting in the grocery line or while getting your hair or toes done, take some time to read. While you're jogging, you could even jog to the tune of an amazing audiobook. You may even want to consider joining a book club. The accountability the group members provide will help you in your journey. Even if it takes you a while to finish a book, it's okay. I promise you, intentionally adding reading time to your schedule will definitely change your life for the better.

The benefits of reading

There are so many benefits to adding reading to your schedule. For starters, reading keeps your mind active. In fact, ABC News did a report on how mentally stimulating activities (such as reading) can decrease your chances of developing Alzheimer's. There are many studies that suggest reading can help improve your memory. My husband's colleague, for example, can remember intimate details about the customers he's served throughout the years. What does he credit it to? Reading!

When you're having a pretty stressful day, reading can help calm you down. Reading gives you the ability to escape your present circumstances. You can become someone new or travel 3,000 miles away—for cheap—and you don't even have to worry about jet lag. My oldest daughter, Faith, likes to practice this technique. For example, when my middle child, Grace, does things to pester her older sister, Faith will sometimes turn to reading to escape the drama. We try to keep as many chapter books from our local library on hand for times like this. I'm glad my daughter has found a positive coping mechanism that will serve her well into the future.

Another benefit of reading is that you can find many answers to problems you're facing. If you've been struggling with something in particular, chances are there's someone else who has been where you are. Reading books about people with similar experiences can give you the chance to see things with a different perspective, and to feel understood by others. It also gives you the chance to see which methods helped others solve their problems. This doesn't mean you have to follow what everyone else is doing. Simply absorb the good information, and apply techniques you feel will work best for your current situation. Regardless of your issues, reading is a great way to help jumpstart your thinking, and to help you reach your goal.

The great thing about reading is that, even if you are unable to attend college or pay for extensive training of any kind, you can still gain expertise by reading books. Don't underestimate the power of self-education. Books and articles hold so much information. The very answer you need for your situation may be waiting for you right between the pages of a book. I'm a firm believer that you can find many answers to your problems by reading.

We've talked about several ways in which reading can help jumpstart your thinking, yet the most obvious reason is because you learn things you never knew. Reading can help you gain more expertise on the Roman Empire or you could learn how to start your own business while working. All of this knowledge helps you develop more of a positive mindset. You begin to let go of old thinking patterns, and you embrace new thoughts that will accelerate your growth, and help you successfully achieve your goal.

Reading creates opportunities

I will preface this section by saying this is not an endorsement of any kind. I chose to speak about this person because he is an example of someone who's personally experienced how reading can create a wealth of opportunities in one's life. Republican presidential candidate Ben Carson grew up in a single-parent home with his brother. His mother worked hard to take care of him and his brother. One common theme Carson's mother found among the wealthy people she worked for was that they preferred reading books to watching television. Even though Carson's mom couldn't read, she made her sons read and submit book reports to her every week. What began as a "chore" grew into something that helped Ben turn his life around.

Prior to reading, Ben struggled in school. However, after developing his new love for reading, he improved his grades, and began to see potential and value in himself. Instead of feeling like he would never get out of poverty, Carson saw the light at the end of the tunnel. Not only did he see a bright future, but he put in the work to make this bright future a reality. Imagine that. Carson was able to use reading as a way to find hope in a seemingly hopeless situation. Just think about what it can do for your life.

Audiobooks, e-books, and hard copies

Technology has made it easier for you to get your hands on a copy of a book. You can listen to a book while driving around town, download a book to your Kindle, or purchase one online or from your local bookstore. Does it really matter which form you choose? Will it impact your ability to reach your goal? In all honesty, it depends on you and your learning style.

Personally, I love audio books when I am unable to read a physical copy. For example, if I am on my way to pick up my children from school or if I am on a long trip, listening to a good audiobook helps me to surround myself with positive vibes. I love the convenience of e-books. When I don't put things back where they belong, I can count on wasting precious minutes of time searching for what I need. Fortunately, I don't have to worry about this with e-books because they're on my Kindle.

With all of the convenience audio books and e-books offer, I must admit that I am "old school" at heart. There is nothing quite like a good, old-fashioned hardback or softback book. I love the feel of the pages between my fingers. Call me crazy, but I feel like I can really relax with a good book in hand. I also love hard copies because I enjoy taking notes with cute, colorful pens, and highlighting important quotes as I read.

The point is this: If you are dedicated to achieving

success, you must work to improve your mindset. You must make time to find books to help you reach your goal. You may be on a budget, and that's okay. Reading doesn't have to be as costly as other forms of entertainment. Head on over to your local library or scour the web for free e-books. You can even exchange books with a friend after you've made a purchase. Even if you're unable to use those awesome glitter or colorful gel pens to help you take notes in books or to highlight your favorite quotes, it is still worth the experience. Simply keep a notebook with all of your "aha" moments you gained from reading. If you want to develop the positive mindset you need to reach your goal, you really cannot afford to forego reading. It's a worthwhile investment in your future.

What should I read?

By now, you know how valuable reading can be to developing a positive mindset. You also know how affordable it can be to maintain your reading habit. Maybe you're wondering what kinds of books you should read. You could start out by reading books that will specifically give you information to help you reach your goal. Ask a librarian or your friends and family for ideas about good books to read. You could also look up best-seller lists to see if there is anything about your interests. Try reading through different genres, and see which one stands out to you the most. Once you start reading, your attitude will improve, and you will see a shift in your thinking.

When choosing a book to read, the most important thing is that the book will add value to your life. You won't be able to jumpstart your thinking and reach your goal if you are reading negative, trashy material. There is enough nonsense going on in the world on a daily basis, there's no need to invite more negativity into your life through reading. This is not to say you can't enjoy a good mystery or romance story. Yet, if you feel the book you're reading is taking your life and thought process in a direction that contradicts your core values, you should reconsider reading it.

Self-Check Guide

Think about your reading habits. Then reflect on and answer the questions below.

1. How often do you read?

2. What type of information do you enjoy reading?

3. How do you feel after reading?

4. How can reading help you reach your goal?

5. What kind of books do you want to start reading?

6. How can you make more time in your schedule for reading?

Call to Action

You learned a lot about the importance of reading, and how it can help you jumpstart your thinking. Your task now is to create a list of books you should read to help you further develop the mindset you need to achieve your goal. Remember, you can ask your family, friends, or local librarian for advice. You can also search the web for ideas. Once you create your list, choose the one that you will start with. Schedule time to read daily—even it's only for a few minutes. It's not about quantity, but quality. Reflect on your readings and engage in discussion about your findings with your accountability partner or someone else who may be interested.

7 IT'S NOT THAT SERIOUS—OR IS IT?

[Film] has the power to cross generations, cross language boundaries, and provoke us to deal with issues in our culture and personal belief system.
-Joe Poe

It takes a lot to develop a positive mindset, and to intentionally work towards reaching your goal. You've learned that there is power in what you say, what you listen to, what you read, and even in how you value yourself. It may seem like a lot to do, but you owe it to yourself to try. There are a few other things you need to consider as you embark on your journey. Let's talk about the next one: television and the film industry.

Have you ever been too afraid to watch a movie your friends wanted to see? They may have told you, "It's just a movie!" I know I've heard that statement so many times before. I used to feel badly for ruining everyone's movie plans. Maybe you have, too. What if I told you your thoughts and beliefs are shaped in part by what you watch?

Watching television and movies can have a profound effect on your mind. There are actually several benefits of watching television and movies. One benefit is its informative or educational appeal. Although reading can use powerful imagery, there is something to be said about the visual stimulation evoked in film and television. As a former teacher, I can recall students being able to understand certain concepts better because of the use of movies or video clips. For example, it can be quite difficult to teach the difference between dramatic, situational and verbal irony without some form of visual representation.

Believe it or not, television and movies can also be beneficial as therapeutic agents. In one of my graduate courses, I was instructed to choose between two different movies, and identify appropriate counseling theories that would have benefited the characters. I also took graduate courses that showed how clients could use film to identify better ways to respond to similar situations in their lives. Some therapists would even agree that making a movie can be therapeutically beneficial because it allows the therapist to see life from the client's perspective. This is a strategy I would definitely like to try one day. I like these activities because they encourage individuals to practice concepts they learned.

Clearly, there are good reasons to watch television and movies. However, if used inappropriately, you could have difficulties achieving success and instead develop a poor perspective of life. For this reason, you must be careful about what you watch. Everyone is different. You know how media affects you. You may be able to entertain certain shows or movies that someone else cannot, and that is okay. Simply take notice of how watching media affects you, and make adjustments as necessary.

How can media affect me?

For years, researchers have known that watching negative images has a negative influence on us. For example, watching movies or television shows with negative themes or images can significantly alter your mood, the way you treat others, the way you view your current circumstances, and even the way you respond in various situations. Take a minute to think about that. When is the last time you watched something that changed you or affected you in a way you didn't think it would? Have you ever responded a certain way based on something you saw on television?

I can remember watching a movie some years ago called *The Ring*. Initially, I didn't seem to have too many issues watching it. Yet, for some reason or another, I had to stop watching scary movies altogether a few years later. I became too fearful and paranoid. It was difficult to be home alone some nights while my husband worked. It was also a bit challenging when I had to drive alone at night. I know you're probably thinking the same thing my husband did: it's just a movie! You know what? I'm sure you're right. I get it—I really do. The point I'm trying to make is that television and movies can influence our thoughts, beliefs, and actions. Amazingly enough, my movie choices were causing me to see things a bit irrationally. I admit there are bad people in the world, but I shouldn't be consumed with the thought that they are lurking around every corner!

Over the years, I've learned that everything is not for everyone. Apparently, I don't do well watching scary movies, among other things. You may have a different set of issues you wrestle with. Maybe certain things bother you now that never did in the past. That's okay. Take this knowledge and use it to help you stay on track to developing a positive mindset and achieving your goal. Resist the urge to allow television or movies to deter you from stepping out on faith and walking into your greatness.

Is no news really good news?

When I was a little girl, I can remember being forced to

watch the local news almost every school morning. My brother and I hated it. We would have preferred to watch cartoons of course. Now that I'm older, I still don't care to watch the news. Although it's informative, I feel so drained and depressed after watching a few of the stories. In fact, researchers estimate that between 47% and 60% of news stories are negative in nature. That's a lot! Oftentimes, these stories affect the psychological state of viewers. With such a high level of negativity portrayed, it's no wonder some individuals battle depression and anxiety. Understandably so, it can be difficult to remain in good spirits after watching so many negative news cycles.

Does this mean you shouldn't watch the news? No, not necessarily. The news can provide much-needed information. Nevertheless, I would advise you to monitor how much and how frequently you watch the news, television programs, movies, music videos, and anything else with negative content. Trust me, I am not telling you to stop watching media! There are so many great things to be learned from watching television. You simply need to be aware of its effect on your psyche and, ultimately, your ability to walk into your greatness.

Persevere!

If you aren't careful, watching negative forms of media can make you begin to believe less in yourself and in your goal. Sometimes you may focus on how well others are doing, and think the world doesn't need to hear your version. You may think you don't have anything additional to offer. You may even feel afraid that you will have a bad experience similar to one that a movie character endured. You are not alone. You would be surprised how many people emulate what they see on television and in film.

So, what does this mean for you? You know what your goal is. You know how important it is to protect that goal. Make intentional choices about what you will allow to shape your mindset. If your choices have a negative effect then make adjustments accordingly.

Self-check Guide

Only you can determine how beneficial or detrimental a television show or movie can be to your life. You know how valuable and harmful media can be to your success. Reflect on the chapter and answer the questions below.

1) How do your television and movie choices affect you emotionally?

2) What are some limiting beliefs you have? Can these be directly or indirectly tied to what you watch?

3) Do your television and movie choices lead you toward or away from your goal?

Call to Action

Reflect on your goal. What are some television and movie choices that may help you move closer to achieving your goal? Watch one that sticks out to you. If you are unsure of what to watch, consider asking friends and family for suggestions. Your local media specialist may be able to assist you, too. Don't forget that you can always use Google for recommendations.

As you watch the show or movie, pay attention to how the characters react to various situations. Can you identify any characters that have overcome limiting beliefs similar to yours? How can you implement some of their strategies to achieve success?

8 THINK AND ACT ON PURPOSE

It's not enough to be busy; so are the ants. The question is: What are we busy about?
-Henry David Thoreau

Oftentimes, many people go throughout their days without a schedule or list of goals that they would like to accomplish. They simply wake up, go to work, and come home. When you ask them how their day went, they say it went well or that it was "just work". And you know what? That may very well be true. They may have met a deadline at work, or avoided telling their boss what they really wanted to say. Yet five, ten, fifteen years go by. These same individuals are in the same spot, and it doesn't seem like much has changed. The question is: what did these individuals really accomplish? They were able to provide for themselves, but they also worked to make someone else's dream come true.

Now, for some people, they may be fine with working a nine to five job for 30 years, and then go on to enjoy retirement. To be honest, there is nothing wrong with that. We all have a purpose. Nevertheless, if you want more out of your life, you must act and think on purpose. While helping someone else achieve their dream, you can also work just as hard to make your dream become a reality. How do you do this? You must make a specific plan and follow through with it. Anyone can make a plan; however, it's the follow through part that gets a lot of us. If you ever expect to reach your goal, you have to learn how to follow through. If not, it's like missing life's easiest layup. Contrary to popular belief, success doesn't happen by chance. After finalizing your strategies, you must work diligently to see your vision come to pass.

I did a little research on some ants, and noticed some interesting things. Ants are a very special kind of insect for several reasons. For starters, there are different types of ants. Every ant has a job in a colony, and each one knows what its job or purpose is in life. Some ants may be responsible for mating with the queen, while others may be responsible for gathering food. Each job is important and necessary—no matter how simple it may seem. Everything an ant does is for the good of the colony. The ant must help the colony survive and thrive. If an ant fails to complete its job, this not only affects that particular ant, but the entire colony.

We have similar characteristics to ants. Like ants, every person was born with a special purpose or job. Every person was also born with a special set of skills or tools to help them achieve their purpose. You may or may not know what your purpose is yet. As you are finding out what you're supposed to do, it's important to remember that, regardless of your purpose or job, you are important. You are special and unique. You matter.

You know what's pretty amazing? Unlike ants, we have the ability to move from worker to queen. What do I mean? For example, a person who grew up in poverty does not have to die in poverty. We are all dealt a certain hand in life. Some may be dealt "better" hands than others, but we all have the choice to play them as we see fit. You see, your thoughts and actions could be holding you back from stepping into your greatness. Let's take a look at an example.

If you don't necessarily have the funding, but still want to open a center for youth living in poverty, you can still do it. How so? You may be thinking, *I don't have the money or influence to do something like that,* or *That sure would be nice if someone else could do it.* Instead of thinking of why you *can't* do something, think of ways you *can.* If you do not learn how to take control of your thoughts and actions, you will have a difficult time in fulfilling your true purpose in life.

Regardless of how many other people see potential in you, it won't mean anything unless *you* see the greatness within you. I've had people tell me that I could make a difference in the lives of many. When some of these people shared what kind of platform they envisioned me using, I admit I had to laugh. I never saw myself making a difference in front of crowds. I never saw myself being in the spotlight. Heck, I never saw myself writing a book, and having people actually buy it! I would rather have been working behind the scenes. It wasn't until I started seeing my potential that good changes started happening. Doors started opening. Possibilities seemed endless. I want you to know the same can happen for you.

You may be reading this now and thinking to yourself, *How can I achieve my goals? How can I make them a reality?* The answer is you have to think and act intentionally. I was listening to the Yolanda Adams Morning Show on the radio one morning, and AV said something that really struck me. He said people often put themselves in cages without realizing it, and they wrestle between fear and frustration. A light bulb immediately went off after I heard those words. I had to evaluate my own life. Would I allow fear and frustration to keep me back from living the life I really wanted and felt I deserved? Will you? If you want to jumpstart your thinking, you must first make up in your mind that *nothing* will stop you from achieving victory.

I truly believe someone reading this book is struggling

with the fear of failure and rejection. I just want you to know that you *can* break free from the chains that are holding you captive. You *can* live the life you want to live and make a difference in the world. The door of your cage is unlocked. What are you going to do about it?

What is your purpose?

This is just my opinion, but I feel like we all are called to be servants—even the wealthiest individuals of this world. That is the first part of our mission and purpose in life. However, the task is to learn and to understand in what capacity you can serve others. Correct me if I'm wrong, but I cannot think of a single job where the employee doesn't provide some form of service towards others. Even the president of a company serves his or her employees. The president cannot earn more money without the help of those employees. Therefore, the president is usually pretty willing to do what it takes to make the employees happy (to a certain degree) because it means he or she will reap a good harvest, too.

You must be sure of your purpose. No one can really tell you what your purpose is or how to carry it out. It is something you learn with experience. Why do I say that? I say it because you don't want to live your life through someone else. When things start to go crazy in your life, you don't want to blame it on following someone else's opinion of your purpose. When things get tough, you want to be able to acknowledge the challenge, and be reminded of why you are on the path you chose. If you aren't sure why you're going a certain route, you need to stop immediately and seek clarity. Why? Because you must be able to think and act intentionally. You must live out your dreams. You cannot do this if you are living based on what someone else said you should do.

When it was time to declare a major for college, I had no idea what I wanted to do. I thought about what I was good at, and what I enjoyed. I had the most amazing

French teacher ever—Madame Black. She had such passion for teaching each and every day. I seriously cannot recall ever seeing her spirits down. I wanted to be just like her and inspire other students. My family wasn't too thrilled with my decision. I mean, they weren't badgering me, but I think they wanted me to do something that would make more money. Now that I have three children, I can completely appreciate why they wanted me to take a different route. Nevertheless, I would not have gained the insights and experiences I now have if I had chosen a different profession.

Although I wasn't meant to stay in a classroom for thirty years, I sincerely appreciate every life lesson I learned while I was there. A few years ago, I probably couldn't have told you that. However, I have grown and now understand the power of developing a positive mindset. Every good and negative experience I endured was simply leading me to a greater calling on my life. You may be feeling the same way today. You may think you will never find out what you are truly supposed to do with your life. I want to encourage you. You weren't meant to stay where you are for forever. Your present circumstances do not dictate your future. So, absorb the positive from every situation, and intentionally use these experiences to propel you into your destiny.

If you want to think better and do better, you must do it intentionally. You cannot achieve success if you are not disciplined, persistent, and consistent. Sure, there will be tough days when you struggle with negativity. There will be days when you feel like you cannot continue on the path to your destiny. Yet you must remember that your thoughts and actions affect those around you. Your dream or goal is not just about you. Don't be selfish about sharing your talents with others. Trust me. Your goal is the answer to the prayers of so many around the world.

Is living aimlessly really dangerous?

Put some action on good intentions.
-Lorii Myers

If you fail to act and think on purpose then you are acting and thinking aimlessly. We have already established that in order to jumpstart your actions and thoughts you must do so intentionally. You may have the best intentions in the world to do better and to be better, but you need to follow through with actions—not words. When I was a little girl, my mom always told me, "Your actions speak louder than your words." Like the ants we referenced earlier, you must have a plan. Your plan must consist of how you want to successfully overcome negative thoughts, actions, and procrastination. If you fail to plan intentional and specific steps to achieve your goals then serious repercussions can happen.

When you do not think or act on purpose, you can begin to feel dissatisfied. For example, you may be unhappy with your career choice because you think you do not have any options that will allow you to do better than what you are already doing. You may have chosen your job as a temporary fix. You may have simply needed something quick to help take care of your family's needs until you could find something better. Yet your "better job" never happened because you did not make intentional steps for it to happen. You cannot expect to find a better paying job without making purposeful decisions and actions.

When you do not think or act on purpose, it can feel as if you are living in a stagnant state of life. Being stagnant is like being stuck in mud—you're not going anywhere. This can make it difficult to grow and to reach your fullest potential in life. I can remember getting frustrated a few years ago. I was married with only two children at the time, working full time as a high school French teacher, and I was completing courses for my

Master's degree in school counseling. Every day seemed like the same unfulfilling story: I woke up, helped my children get ready for school, went to work, helped my children with homework after school, prepared dinner, put my children to bed, worked on homework for grad school, showered, and went to bed. This was my schedule day in and day out. It was very monotonous and boring. I told my husband one day that there had to be more to life than what we were experiencing at the time. I felt so trapped and stagnant in my personal and professional growth. I was wandering through life aimlessly.

You may be thinking, *Hey, you had a good career with benefits, and you were working on another degree. You had a great future ahead of you.* I'll tell you this: even though I was working on a degree, and I had a pretty good job, I still wasn't sure what to do with the rest of my life. Heck, I didn't even know how I would make it through the next five to ten years.

My brain was all over the place. I was very dissatisfied with the direction my life was heading, and I wanted so much more for my family and myself. Maybe you feel the same way. Maybe you feel you have no direction in life. Maybe you have an idea of what you want to do, but you don't know how to get there. I want to encourage you to sit down, and write out your goals. Although your goals should be achievable, do not put yourself in a box. Then you need to focus on one goal at a time. Write down the short-term goals you need to accomplish in order to make your long-term goal an actual success. If you try to achieve everything at once you will be overwhelmed, and will likely quit.

Although you've committed to taking steps to live and think on purpose, opposition will surely come. The truth is you can't control the hand that is dealt you. However, regardless of how many negative thoughts penetrate your mind, you can choose to see the value, the lessons, and the good in everything! In order to jumpstart your thinking and actions, you must constantly choose to think and do positive things. You really do have a choice. The ball is in your court.

Do I really have a choice?

Happiness is a conscious choice, not an automatic response.
-Mildred Barthel

When I was a little girl, I hated making mistakes because I didn't want my parents to be mad at me. Sometimes, I wondered if they still loved me after I did bad things. Now, of course, my parents loved me—how could they not? (Smile, Mom and Dad!) Yet, somehow, I took their chastisement as an indication that something was terribly wrong with me, and that I couldn't be loved anymore. I used to think things like, *Well, I've failed them again,* or *I can't ever do anything right.* See how easy it is to have and accept negative thoughts as truth? My parents never did anything to make me feel unloved, yet I *chose* to think the worst at times.

You may be suffering from the horrible effects of negative thoughts, too. Maybe you think you're not good enough to be in a relationship with someone. Maybe you don't think you're smart enough to go to college or to start your own business. Someone may have told you that you would never make it. They said you would never do or be anything special.

I'll be honest with you. It really sucks when you feel like other people do not believe in you or that no one cares about you. Sometimes we insist that other people view us negatively when, in fact, this is far from the truth. And then, unfortunately, there are times when it *is* true that others do not like us for any number of reasons. What I want you to understand is that, in order to jumpstart your thinking, you have to know who you are, know your purpose, make intentional steps to achieve your goal, and stop caring about who does or does not support you. Don't just think about how cool it would be to make your dream a reality. You need to also create a solid plan, and act accordingly.

Remember how we talked about the importance of speaking positively? If you find yourself being bombarded with these negative thoughts, you have the power to intentionally speak life into your situation. Repeat after me: "I am smart. I am attractive. I have a thriving business. I attract money wherever I go. My bank account balance is increasing daily. I am happy. I am free. I am loved." As I stated earlier, the more you speak positively, the easier it will be to believe what you're saying. Intentionally thinking and doing positive things can be difficult initially, but you can do it. It's your choice.

Self-Check Guide

If you haven't had a chance to do some reflection, think about what you want out of life. As you're reflecting, answer the questions below.

1) What goal do you want to focus on first? Remember, it is easier to accomplish one goal at a time.

2) What steps have you taken so far to achieve this goal?

3) Have your actions been helping you achieve your goal?

4) If your actions haven't helped you achieve your goal, what can you do differently? Write these steps down. These will serve as short-term goals that will lead to the completion of your long-term goal.

5) How will you address negative thoughts that come to you during your journey?

Call to Action

I want you to keep your answers from the self-check guide. Review these answers weekly until you reach your goal. This will serve as a gentle reminder that you can achieve anything with the right planning, thinking, and action.

9 DID I DO THAT?

The moment you take responsibility for everything in your life is the moment you can change anything in your life.
-Hal Elrod

In order to achieve success and jumpstart your thinking, you must embrace accountability. Now, this can be a difficult thing to do at times. Trust me, no one wants to be responsible for burning the Thanksgiving turkey or for being the reason the family missed their flight. In these moments, it feels like we are wearing an invisible dunce hat or a scarlet letter for the entire world to see. Yet, when we are accountable, we realize how unfair it would be to blame anyone else for our limitations or failures except us. When we are late to an appointment, we shouldn't blame it on traffic or anyone else. Sure, traffic may be a little heavier than usual, but I'm sure that's not the *only* reason why you're late. Take responsibility by admitting you could have left home earlier if you hadn't been catching up on the latest episode of your favorite television program or catching five more minutes of an awesome nap.

The same logic can be applied to our thoughts. We must accept responsibility for the thoughts we entertain.

For example, my husband and I became pregnant six months after we got married. Everything was great during the pregnancy. I really couldn't have had a better first time experience. Yet, after I delivered, my thoughts about my body worsened. I mean, I never really had great self-esteem anyway, but it really got worse after giving birth.

As many mothers know, pregnancy changes your body in ways you never thought possible—and I'll leave it at that! Sometimes, I secretly thought my husband would start looking at other women because my body was no longer the same—insane, I know. So, when my husband would tell me how beautiful he thought I was, I automatically rejected it. Without knowing it, I was feeding into the vicious, negative self-esteem cycle I'd battled for so many years. Yet, it was no one's fault but my own. I couldn't blame anyone else for my choice to entertain those crazy, irrational thoughts.

Now, you may have a different story than mine. Maybe you are filling your head with lies about your talents, your intellect, or even about how awful you foresee your future. Regardless of what anyone else has said or done to you, you must take responsibility for your share in the negativity. Being brutally honest with yourself is not always easy, but it is necessary if you want to change your thinking habits.

You may be thinking that this journey to developing a positive mindset is too difficult. You may be thinking you'll always be where you currently are in life. I don't know how many of you have ever heard of Joyce Meyer. I'm not sure if many would call her a preacher or pastor since she doesn't have a church, but, nonetheless, she is an amazing, radical speaker and author. Some of you may not know that she was also molested for years by her father. Now, she could have allowed that horrific moment to shatter her for the remainder of her life. She could have chosen to live in the past, but she didn't. She went on to marry the love of her life, have four children, and grow her ministry as a powerful, dynamic female evangelist. Truth be told, I am still in awe of how forgiving she was towards her family in spite of what she went through. What an inspiration she is for us all.

How did she do it? How did Joyce Meyer conquer her dark past? With her faith in God, of course, but she also had to *want* to change her thinking. Holding on to negative thoughts is like ingesting poison, and expecting it not to hurt you. Although Joyce Meyer did not deserve to be raped, she realized that if she chose to hold on to anger and shame, she could never rise to the level of life she wanted. She decided to be accountable for how her thoughts would shape her, and make intentional steps towards thinking more positively. It's not easy, but if Joyce Meyer could do it then so can you and I.

To Do or Not to Do

It is not only what we do, but also what we do not do for which we are accountable.
-Jean Baptiste Molière

In order to jumpstart your thinking, you must be accountable for *not* doing what you should be doing. Oftentimes, we look around and wonder how so many other people are living their dream. We wonder how they can be happy and free. Sometimes, we even envy them, their lifestyle, and their accomplishments. Take Beyoncé for example. She is gorgeous, beyond talented, and is extremely wealthy. I mean, who hasn't felt even the tiniest ounce of jealousy against Queen Bey? Yet, how many of us can say we are willing to walk a mile in her shoes?

It is easy to give "reasons" for not doing something. I am guilty of it, too. This is not the first time I've tried to write a book. In fact, I still have a partial book saved on my computer from almost five years ago. One of my "reasons" for never finishing is because I felt I never had the time or I was too tired after getting up so early, working, and taking care of my responsibilities at home. Yet, what was I doing every Thursday night at ten o'clock in the fall and spring? Watching Scandal! Now, don't get me wrong. I will continue to reserve my one night of television per week (on Thursdays, of course); however, I have now learned the value in setting priorities. If I can faithfully sit up late enough to watch an episode of my favorite show then I can faithfully choose one or two nights per week to work on writing more books. It's that simple.

Surprisingly enough, I didn't learn the value of prioritizing and being accountable earlier in life. I have always been a "grandma's girl". My grandma is one of the most caring and supportive people I know, but she is not afraid to tell you the truth. I can remember complaining about not having something I wanted when I was little. Do you know what my grandma told me? "Girl, you gotta learn how to take what you got, and make what you want!" This philosophy has really resonated with me lately. It has also helped me to change my perspective on various circumstances in my life.

As I reflect on my journey with this book, I realize how true my grandma's words are. For starters, I did not have a huge budget to work with. I could not afford to purchase a high quality website with all of the bells and whistles. I could not afford to pay for a ton of advertising, and so much more. I could have chosen once again to dream but not take the necessary steps to making that dream a reality. Yet, I am so glad I chose to persevere in spite of what looked like too much of a challenging situation.

I challenge each of you to be more positive and accountable for your actions. Even when it does not seem like your dream is possible, act as if it is anyway! Remember, your small steps will lead to your greatness. You'll be surprised at how many doors will open to help you achieve your dream if only you take responsibility for your part.

Why do I need an accountability partner?

As iron sharpens iron, so a friend sharpens a friend.
-Proverbs 27:17 New Living Translation

Many coaches tell their team, "There is no 'I' in TEAM." One person cannot expect to play every position effectively. With all due respect, even the great Michael Jordan needed the help of his team to earn his six championship rings. Sometimes players get tired, and need assistance. Sometimes, they also need to be able to recognize when they need the help of someone who is stronger or someone who has more expertise. You can apply the same principal to your goal. It is much easier to accomplish your goal if you have a support partner or group consisting of positive individuals—"go getters". These individuals should be willing to help you remain accountable for the successes *and* failures you encounter on your journey.

When looking for someone to be your accountability partner, think of it like a job search. Create a list of characteristics and qualities this person should have. You should be compatible enough to work with this individual. However, I must warn you: your accountability partner should not be there to simply agree with everything you say. They need to be as tough as nails, and push you to reach your goals—even when you don't want to go on anymore. If you choose to solicit help from a family member or close friend, please make sure they are truly supportive and understanding of your goal. Remember, NOT everyone wants to see you succeed—even those closest to you.

If you are financially able to do so, you should consider investing in a personal coach or mentor. You can also join paid accountability groups. Facebook allows you to join and create paid groups that are filled with like-minded individuals to help you reach your goal, too. Now you may be thinking, *Why would I ever choose to pay someone to help me be accountable? Isn't willpower enough? I can do this on my own.* The truth is if you have to pay for services, you are usually more likely to take your goal seriously. Your goal becomes more than just a hobby you do in your spare time; it actually means something to you now that you've placed a dollar value on it. An accountability partner or group is not responsible for your results, but is there to help you manage the issues that arise on your journey.

So, are accountability partners or coaches really worth the investment? Well, that depends on your perception. Personally, I believe there are so many reasons why you should consider having a coach or support group. For instance, it is quite helpful to have someone there as a sounding board. As I mentioned earlier, you cannot do everything as effectively as others could. By accepting a fresh perspective, you could find different ways to help you reach your goal faster. Throughout the entire process, your trusted coach or support group can cheer you on and give you the emotional support you need.

There are other reasons why you should consider an accountability partner or group. They can help you have a higher chance of reaching your goal. How so? It's easy to give in to our emotions and quit when "the grits hits the fan" so to speak. We've all been there. Yet, our beloved support system will be right there to pull us back to reality. They will help us guard against complacency, and fearlessly point out our limitations. In some ways, they are the glue that holds us together on our journey. Some people are alarmed by the cost of these types of services. However, I like to look at it as an investment that will give back to you—unlike the latest purse or piece of technology.

Self-Check Guide

Being accountable is not always easy, but it is necessary for your growth and success. Reflect on and respond to the questions below to assess how you can improve your level of accountability.

1) When was the last time you blamed someone else for something that happened? Think about this situation and assess your actions that contributed to the outcome.

2) Why do you think you struggle with being accountable?

3) What action steps can you take to become more accountable in all areas of your life?

Call to Action

The first step to solving your problem is to admit that you have a problem. Reflect on your answer to question number two. Honesty brings humility. Do not feel badly about your limitations. Everyone has an area in their life that could be improved.

Now, weigh the benefits of having a paid/free accountability group or mentor. If you decide to use free services that is fine. Think of individuals in your life you would like to serve as your accountability partner(s) or mentor. Now write down the names of your top choices, and list the qualities that make each person stand out as a good candidate to keep you accountable. Then you need to choose which person(s) you need to ask to serve as your accountability partner(s).

If you choose to use paid services, research and compare the information you gather. Write down the names you found and list why you would consider each group or person. Most coaches and mentors have a free discovery call to see if you would be an ideal candidate for their services. Find out how you can contact the person(s) of interest to you. Make an appointment to speak with him or her, and decide if you are compatible enough to work together to make your dream a reality.

10 HI. I'M A RECOVERING PERFECTIONIST.

Perfectionism doesn't make you feel perfect, it makes you feel inadequate.
-Maria Shriver

Has anyone ever told you that in order to be successful you have to be perfect? The truth is we look at people we feel fit our ideal of what it means to be perfect, and we measure our actions against theirs. I want to let you in on a secret though. Are you paying attention? Read this next sentence carefully. There is no rule book that says you must be perfect in order to be considered a successful person. Seriously, this rule book doesn't exist. We run into problems when we fail to live up to the ridiculous standards we placed on ourselves. We feel like failures. We begin to think, *What went wrong? Why can't my life be perfect like theirs?* In order to be happy with your success and embrace a positive outlook, you have to let go of perfectionism.

There are definitely serious dangers to embracing perfectionism. One danger is that you risk dying without ever realizing how incredible you truly are. Perfectionists tend to focus on what they do not do well instead of their successes. That's unfortunate. An unknown person once said, "A perfectionist pardons everyone's mistakes but his own." This quote really resonates with me because I am, in fact, in a recovering perfectionist.

I don't know why, but I've struggled quite a bit with perfectionism since childhood. For some reason, I had it in my head that more people would love me if I was perfect. I also thought I would seem more important and valuable to others if I could only be perfect. The crazy thing is I don't feel that way about other people, meaning, although I can be critical of others, I am honestly more critical of myself. It drives me insane to see errors in my work because, to me, it is always supposed to be professional or "A grade" quality work. I guess I've taken to the extreme certain things I learned as a child. For instance, outward appearances have always been important to my family. Therefore, it always meant a lot to put my "best foot forward". Yet, as I said before, I am a work in progress. I have definitely let go of a lot of things over the past few years.

Another danger to being a perfectionist is that you jeopardize your happiness. It's hard for perfectionists to really enjoy anything because mistakes stick out like a sore thumb. I can remember going on trips with my family, and having such a horrible time. Everyone else seemed to be having the time of their lives, but I couldn't stop thinking about how I left the snack bag on the dining room table. I cannot imagine how many great memories I missed out on because of my struggle with perfectionism. Thank God for change!

Taming the Perfectionist in You

I am careful not to confuse excellence with perfection. Excellence, I can reach for: perfection is God's business.
       -Michael J. Fox

You may be wondering if it is really possible to tame the perfectionist in you. The optimist in me reassures me that one day I will finally be completely free from my perfectionist tendencies. In the meantime, I am a living witness that you can make steps to control this obsessive compulsive behavior. Trust me; every day is a new opportunity to do better than you did the day before. Some days, I have to work harder than others. For example, my husband is a furniture store manager. When I go to visit him, you would not believe how much I have to fight the urge sometimes to refrain from straightening pillows on every couch and bed. My husband laughs, but the struggle is real some days.

I have decided to refuse to allow perfectionism to keep me from being successful and maintaining a positive outlook. If you feel the same way, I hope you benefit from the three things that help me combat perfectionism. The first thing I do is set realistic expectations for myself. I may need to redefine my perspective occasionally, but I notice such a difference when I do not impose insane requirements on myself. When my to-do list is realistic, I feel more successful because I am truly capable of accomplishing each of the tasks. When I feel successful, I tend to think more positively about my capabilities. It's all circular.

Another thing that helps me combat perfectionism is celebrating small successes. In the past, I often felt extremely overwhelmed and stressed. Why? Because I looked at the "big picture" instead of trying to look at things in smaller parts. By focusing on smaller, achievable goals, I can truly feel successful. It is this attitude I used to write this book. Writing a book used to seem like an impossible task. However, I saw more and more success with the completion of each chapter. Why? Because I knew that each chapter brought me closer to finishing. Is every chapter "perfect"? No. I'm sure I could have elaborated more in certain places or made other changes. However, it's like the old saying goes: done is better than perfect. If you want to feel more successful, open your eyes to the good in you and in your actions. Learn to celebrate your small successes just as much as the huge ones.

The last tip I keep in mind to combat perfectionism is to love myself for who I am. This may be hard to do initially for some. However, I challenge you to see the beauty in yourself—especially in your imperfections. It is essential to love and accept yourself for who you are if you want to truly enjoy your success. You can't have a positive outlook on life while maintaining a negative view of yourself. Don't be overwhelmed by how many issues you think you have. Simply try to love yourself more today than you did yesterday.

Self-Check Guide

It is incredible to think about how many people suffer from perfectionism. So many people we consider to be successful have difficulties in truly enjoying their success because of irrational expectations. The great news is that you don't have to suffer for the rest of your life from this unhealthy perspective. There is hope! Reflect on and answer the questions below to help you enjoy your successes and jumpstart your thinking.

1) Are you a perfectionist?

2) What issues do you believe you have? In other words, what do you view as your imperfections?

3) Why do you feel the need to be perfect?

4) Do you experience difficulty enjoying your successes?

5) What steps can you take to celebrate your successes (especially the small ones!)?

Call to Action

Think back to how beneficial affirmations can be for your life. In this activity, you will need paper and a pen or pencil—unless you're too techy for that! Your task is to write a letter to yourself. In this letter, you need to compliment your physical looks, intelligence, heart, personality, accomplishments, abilities, and anything else that will remind you of why you are perfect just the way you are. You are exquisite. You do not need to change or be like anyone else in order to seem successful. It can be difficult to compliment yourself at first, but this is such a necessary activity on your journey to jumpstarting your thinking.

10 CAN'T STOP, WON'T STOP

Perseverance is failing 19 times and succeeding the 20th.
-Julie Andrews

I come from a family of military men. My dad was a Marine, and my brother is an active Airman. As civilians, we often go about our lives without much thought to the dangers and challenges our service men and women encounter on a daily basis. Nevertheless, there is so much we can learn from their lifestyle. For example, soldiers are strong, disciplined, courageous, and they take action.

There are times when soldiers are instructed to complete a mission that may seem near impossible. There may be missions where a group is outnumbered, lacks sufficient protection, or where there is imminent danger. Does the goal of the mission change simply because they encounter obstacles? No. Even if a group of soldiers must regroup or try a different tactic, the goal of the mission does not change. In the face of fear and danger, the soldiers must still move forward.

You can apply these same strategies as you embark upon your journey. I don't know what led you to develop a negative mindset, but I do know you can learn to replace those poisonous thoughts with positive ones. I must be honest with you, however, about one thing: when you truly make up your mind that you are absolutely 100% committed to developing a positive mindset and achieving your goal, you will be faced with a lot of opposition. Believe me, I do not say this to scare you. Instead, I'm saying this to prepare you for what is surely to come. When you finally decide that you will do whatever it takes to make a change in your life and achieve your goal, simply be prepared to overcome some challenges along the way.

As you begin your journey, things may seem to be going quite well initially. You are ready to conquer the world because you have a rock solid plan in place, and you are committed to doing the work. As time goes on, do not be surprised if you see changes in your personal and professional life. Small problems or fires may arise. Don't worry; you will put them out successfully. Then, all of a sudden, you will have days where it seems like absolutely nothing can go right. There will be days when it seems like fire and brimstone are surrounding you. You may feel like there isn't anything you could possibly salvage from your day.

It's funny how things can be going so great one day and then, all of a sudden, the floodgates open. Some friends and family members who seemed to have believed in you from the beginning start to change. They suddenly don't see your vision. They begin to compare you to others and question if you can really compete. You may even have drama starting in your own household. You may not understand why petty arguments are increasing, or why your children can't seem to get it together lately. You may find your finances taking more unexpected hits. One day your tires blow out, and the next day you find out you need a new water pump. It seems as if you are going to run out of money and won't be able to fund your dream.

Here comes the rush of negative thoughts. Maybe the

unexpected challenges are signs you should give up on trying to make a lifestyle change. Should you really continue working towards your goal? Was your dream really given to you? Have you been wasting your time? Did you really hear what you thought you heard before embarking on this crazy journey?

As crazy as things are going, you simply need to walk in faith. You know what you heard. That dream was placed inside of you for a reason. That goal was given to you for a specific purpose. You were specifically designed and created to overcome every obstacle that is placed in front of you. You *will* come out on top! You may go through the fire, but you will come out as pure gold. There is no doubt about it. You just need to hold to your vision until it is completed.

Although you will have your share of difficulties to overcome, just know that you are not alone. Every person with a successful business and life endured countless roadblocks; however, they persevered. That's what you will need to do in order to achieve your greatness. Continue to say your affirmations—morning, noon, and night. Continue to read positive literature, and listen to positive speakers and podcasts. Continue watching uplifting videos and documentaries. Continue striving to think and act intentionally. By doing so, you will face your fears and obstacles head on. You will become stronger and gain more confidence. You will achieve the greatness you were destined to walk in.

Personal Confession

[35] Do not, therefore, fling away your [fearless] confidence, for it has a glorious *and* great reward. [36] For you have need of patient endurance [to bear up under difficult circumstances without compromising], so that when you have carried out the will of God, you may receive *and* enjoy to the full what is promised.
-Hebrews 10: 35-36 AMP

I must confess that, even as I wrote this book, I encountered some of the same things I talked about earlier in this chapter. It seemed as if the closer I got to my deadline, the more I faced negative thoughts and challenges in my personal life. There were consecutive days when nothing seemed to go right. I could have given up, but what helped me was reading Hebrews 10:35-36, the key verses from my devotional one morning. Those verses spoke life into my very soul and reaffirmed that I was heading down the right path. The more I focused on those verses, the better my day became. I regained control, and managed to get back on track to finishing this book. During other times, it helped to increase my prayers and intentionally surround myself with positivity (i.e. music, podcasts). Most of all, I found it extremely important to always believe that my present struggles were an indication that my victory was surely soon to come.

If I could overcome my obstacles and reach my goal, then you should trust that you can, too. Don't give into the traps that were set to stop you from reaching your goal. There *is* hope for you. Every opposition that is coming against you will fail if you maintain your focus. You may need to take more time to pray and meditate or to readjust your strategy as needed. The only reason you are being fought and challenged so much is because you are about to step into your greatness. You have to trust that, as you continue to develop your positive mindset, you will notice that things will eventually begin to fall into place. Success is waiting for you.

What if I fail?

I can accept failure, everyone fails at something. I can't accept not trying.
-Michael Jordan

You may be wondering what will happen if you fail one day, and give in to the negative thoughts. What will happen if you stumble and let your guard down? The answer is that there is still hope for you. Hopefully, you will learn from your mistakes. You must remember that there is a lesson to be learned in every part of your journey.

It is unfortunate that not everyone is quite as forgiving when you fall short. It's sad, but there are some people who would be happy to see you focus on negative thoughts. Quite honestly, they don't believe in themselves, and they don't want anyone else around them to succeed either. If this happens, it is a reminder that they should be doing better. Yet, when you concentrate on your mistakes, you take your eyes off of the prize. You get off track. In times like this, you need to acknowledge the error, take away something positive from the experience, brush off the dirt, and then keep it moving. In order to be successful and jumpstart your thinking, you can't give up!

The only way you will not learn from your mistakes or achieve your goal is if you to decide to quit. Remember, you have everything you need inside of you to prosper. If you want to be positive then do it. If you want to reach your goal then do it. The only thing stopping you from achieving success is *you*.

Self-Check Guide

1) What challenges have you experienced so far on your journey to developing a positive mindset?

2) How have you overcome some of these challenging moments?

3) How do you plan on addressing moments when you do not stay on track?

4) What lessons have you learned from your failures?

Call to Action

You can learn a lot about yourself from reflecting on how you respond to failure. Begin a journal in which you make notation of how you respond to challenges on your journey. Critique your actions. Praise yourself for good decisions, and write down suggestions for how to handle situations better in the future. Review your journal periodically.

CONCLUSION

I am humbled and honored that you took the time to read this book. I truly believe it is not an accident that you chose to read this. Although not every tip given may necessarily apply to you and your situation, I am confident you were able to take away something that will help propel you into your success. You are now equipped and armed with knowledge that will help not only you on your journey, but those around you as well. Remember, everything you learn is not for you to keep. Instead, pass along knowledge that will help others grow, too.

There was a lot of information covered in this book. Did I expect you to have "arrived" by the conclusion of this book? No. Trust me, none of us has "arrived". My goal was to help you jumpstart your thinking so that you can achieve the success that you truly deserve. My goal was to help you and inspire you as you go throughout your journey. My goal was to remind you of the need to believe in yourself and in the dream that you threw away so long ago. Yeah, that one you never told anyone about. My goal was to remind you that that goal or dream was given to you for a specific purpose and for a specific time. That time is now. It is now time for you to walk into your greatness. It is now time for you to walk into your destiny.

You may feel anxious about how to successfully apply what you learned. You may even have questions about how to implement some of the strategies throughout the book. Remember the old saying, "Rome wasn't built in a day"? Well, neither can you effectively apply all of these tips to your life in one day. Life is like an ocean; it is in constant motion. However, with dedication and the right strategy in place, you will be able to conquer your fears, let go of doubts, and successfully reach your goal. I challenge you to embrace the journey, and love every minute of it.

So, how are you going to do it? I mean how are you really going to change your mindset and achieve the success you truly deserve? You have to decide in your mind that you actually want to change, and that you want to increase your success. Then you have to know who you are and what you're worth. This will give you the solid foundation you need to withstand every challenge that will come before you.

Knowing how to seek the face of the Creator (if you're a believer) or establishing a life of meditation will provide you the communication lines you need to continuously enjoy success on your journey. Recognizing and identifying those things in your life that are blocking you or have blocked you from success will provide you the awareness you need to eliminate those issues. Knowing the importance in guarding who you listen to, what you listen to, what you read, what you say, what you do, and how you plan and live your life will help improve your thinking and maximize your success. Lastly, letting go of the idea that you have to be perfect in order to be successful is crucial. No one would ever have seen this book if I had waited for my version of "perfect" to come about!

All of the tips in this book are necessary as you travel on your journey to achieving success and to developing your new, stronger, and positive mindset. I believe in you. I believe you are fearless and more than capable of success. I believe you are a warrior, a conqueror. I also believe that nothing and no one will stand in the way of you obtaining your goal. Why? Because you now have the necessary tools to develop a strong belief system that cannot be broken. So go out and make that dream a reality. You deserve it!

REFERENCES

Bible Gateway. **Amplified Bible.** Copyright © 2015 by The Lockman Foundation, La Habra, CA 90631. All rights reserved.

Biography.com Editors. Bill Gates (n.d.). Retrieved from http://www.biography.com/people/bill-gates-9307520#early-career on September 26, 2015.

Biography.com Editors. Tyra Banks (n.d.). Retrieved from http://www.biography.com/people/tyra-banks-16242328#video-gallery on September 16, 2015.

Michael Hyatt (2013). *The Secret to Ben Carson's Success. Hint: You Can Use It in Your Life, Too!* Retrieved from http://michaelhyatt.com/ben-carson-reading.html#more-31086 on September 18, 2015. Used by permission. Originally published at www.michaelhyatt.com.

WebMD (2004). Movie Therapy: Using Movies for Mental Health. Retrieved from http://www.webmd.com/mental-health/features/movie-therapy-using-movies-for-mental-health?page=3 on September 27, 2015.

Reading, Chess May Help Fight Alzheimer's (n.d.). Retrieved from http://abcnews.go.com/Health/story?id=117588&page=1 on September 10, 2015.

Szabo, A., & Hopkinson, K. L. (2007). Negative Psychological Effects of Watching the News in the Television: Relaxation or Another Intervention May Be Needed to Buffer Them! *International Journal Of Behavioral Medicine*, *14*(2), 57-62. doi:10.1080/10705500701331170

WHAT PEOPLE ARE SAYING

This is one of the most direct, most effective approaches to helping people achieve their highest potential and continuously expand. Author JaQuette M. S. Gilbert's out-of-the-box strategies for overcoming self-imposed limitations will help anyone who's willing to get out of their own way and walk the path of greatness. No matter where you are, the treasures in this book will guide you to the next level in the game of life so you can win bigger than you ever have before. As I immersed myself in the wisdom of each page, I was reminded that there will always be a calling for each of us to do more, have more, and be more. I want to thank you so much for sharing your experience and insight on how to continuously challenge and stretch beyond the comfort of familiarity in order to live a life of purpose and contribution.

Kevin Brown
Author, Educational Consultant, Entrepreneur
My Conversation with Life

JaQuette Gilbert kudos to you!!! You are the true answer to a few of my prayers! *11 Ways to Jumpstart Your Thinking* is a must read. For anyone who has an overactive thought space or even someone such as I do who has battled anxiety, this is a great resource in showing how to train your mind to respond to things that happen around you. This will equip you with the tools that are needed to recharge the parts of your mind that have been overworked and retrain you to think into existence what you truly desire!

Schericka Posh Chick Gee
Founder and owner of A PoshChick! Events and SheHustles Clothing

11 Ways to Jumpstart Your Thinking is a great tool for someone who wants to be phenomenal but is fighting one of the biggest battles ever...the battle of the mind. JaQuette does a great job by breaking down the steps to break the mind barriers that stop most from pursuing and living their true dreams!

Natasha 'Tottie' Weston
Author & Founder of Confessions of an Ambitious Girl
ConfessionsofanAmbitiousGirl.com

ABOUT THE AUTHOR

JaQuette Gilbert found it alarming that many people are simply "making it" in life instead of living to achieve their dream. Inspired in part by Urie Bronfenbrenner's ecological theory, JaQuette chose to write *11 Ways to JumpStart Your Thinking* as a source of tips to help individuals finally achieve their dream.

JaQuette received her undergraduate degree from Clemson University, and is currently pursuing a Master's degree at Capella University. She worked for eight years as a high school teacher, and now uses her skills to help others strategize and create a plan that will lead to the successful attainment of their goal. JaQuette blogs at joyfullyj.co and can be found on Periscope, Facebook, Twitter, Instagram, and Pinterest @mrsjpgilbert.

JaQuette is a native of Charleston, SC. She now resides in Columbia, SC with her husband, Greg, and their three daughters, Faith, Grace, and Madison. JaQuette enjoys spending time with her family, singing, playing board games, eating warm apple pie, and sipping hot Earl Grey tea—with a spot of sugar and milk of course!

www.ingramcontent.com/pod-product-compliance
Lightning Source LLC
LaVergne TN
LVHW051151080426
835508LV00021B/2572